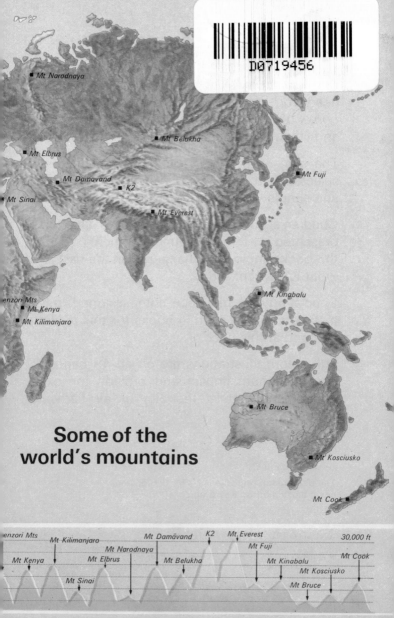

Some of the world's mountains

to teachers and parents

This is a LADYBIRD LEADER book, one of a series specially produced to meet the very real need for carefully planned *first information books* that instantly attract enquiring minds and stimulate reluctant readers.

The subject matter and vocabulary have been selected with expert assistance, and the brief and simple text is printed in large, clear type.

Children's questions are anticipated and facts presented in a logical sequence. Where possible, the books show what happened in the past and what is relevant today.

Special artwork has been commissioned to set a standard rarely seen in books for this reading age and at this price.

Full colour illustrations are on all 48 pages to give maximum impact and provide the extra enrichment that is the aim of all Ladybird Leaders.

Acknowledgments

The photograph opposite is by Mr G H Towers;
cover illustration by Roy Smith.

A Ladybird Leader

mountains

by P H Armstrong B Sc M A Ph D
with illustrations by Gerald Witcomb M SIAD

Ladybird Books Ltd Loughborough 1977

What is a mountain?

A mountain is steep land
that stands out clearly
above the land around it.

Sometimes it is said
that *mountains* are more than
305 metres (1,000 ft)
above sea level,
while *hills* are lower than this.

Mountain Range

Foothills

A group of several mountains
is called a *mountain range*.
The highest point of a mountain
is called the *summit*.

Summit

Plain

How mountains form

Some mountains were formed
by the folding of rocks
that were once beneath the sea.

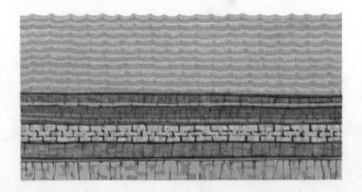

When the rocks were pushed up,
new land formed.

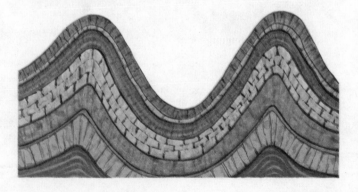

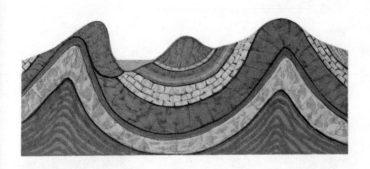

Rain, frost and rivers
gradually wear the land away
over thousands of years.

Sometimes deep *valleys* cut by rivers
run through mountain ranges.

Mountain weather

It is very cold far above sea level,
so on very high mountains
summers are short.

Often it is very windy
close to the summits.

Mountain ranges sometimes have
more rain than lower ground nearby.

When a high mountain
reaches into the clouds,
someone standing on the summit
would be surrounded by mist.

Plant-life on mountains

Because it gets wetter and colder
as one goes higher,
different plants grow
at different heights
on a high mountain.

In the Rocky Mountains
of the south west USA
cacti grow in the deserts
of the foothills.

Higher up are pine and spruce forests.

Above them grow only a few
rock plants, mosses and grasses.

There are patches of snow
on the highest mountains
all through the year.

feet	metres	
		Rock and Snow
13000	3960	
		Grasses and Mosses
11000	3350	
		Fir and Spruce Forest
9000	2740	
		Pine Forest
6500	1980	
		Desert with Cactus and Salt Bush
up to 2000	610	

Plant-life on mountains in south west U S A

Alpine plants

Rock plants or *alpine plants* are small
(they are named after the Alps,
the range of high mountains
in southern Europe)
and often grow
in cracks in the rocks.

Some are like pin-cushions
so that they are not blown to pieces
by the strong winds.

They can survive the cold winters
of high mountains.

Many rock plants have
very beautiful flowers.

13

Mountain animals

Animals that live
in mountainous areas
are very sure-footed
and can climb over rocky ground.

Chamois

Ibex

Bighorn Sheep

Ibex and chamois (say sham-wa)
are among those
that live in the Alps,
and bighorn sheep graze
in the Rocky Mountains.

Alpine meadows

On the mountainsides of the Alps
and some other mountain ranges
alpine pasture is found.

These grassy areas are
full of flowers in summer.

Sheep and goats often graze there.
In Switzerland and Norway
some people live in little houses
high in the mountains in summer.
In winter they take their animals
down to a village.

The advancing snout
of a glacier
in the Rocky Mountains,
Canada

18

Snow-fields and glaciers

On the very highest mountains,
close to the summits
of the Himalayas,
Alps and Rockies,
snow-fields are found.

Sometimes more snow falls in winter
than melts in summer.

As layers of snow press
on those below, ice is formed.

This ice moves downhill as a *glacier*.

Glaciers in Britain

In time glaciers can wear away
(erode) great masses of rock.

Thousands of years ago
in the Ice Age
there were more glaciers
than there are today.

They filled many of the valleys
in the mountains
of northern England, Scotland,
Ireland and Wales.

*Glacial erosion formed
this typical U-shaped
valley*

Volcanoes

Volcanoes such as
Mount Hekla in Iceland
and Mount Fuji in Japan
are mountains that have formed
where *lava* or hot, molten rock
has come from inside the earth
and then cooled to form solid rock.

Often there is a deep, round crater
instead of a summit.

Mt Fuji, Japan

*Close-up of crater
at summit*

More volcanoes

Volcanoes that *erupt*,
throwing out lava
and clouds of ash from time to time,
are called *active* volcanoes.

Those that have not erupted
for many years
are said to be *dormant* (sleeping).
They may erupt again one day.
Extinct or dead volcanoes are those
that have not erupted
for thousands of years.

*A typical extinct
volcano in France*

*Treak Cliff Cavern,
Derbyshire, U K*

Inside mountains

It is sometimes possible
to go inside mountains.

Some rocks are dissolved by water,
so that caves are formed.

Wookey Hole in Somerset
and Treak Cliff Cavern in Derbyshire
are well known English caves.

This painting of a bull was painted 15,000 years ago
in a cave at Lascaux, France

Long ago men lived in caves.

In France and Spain and other places
they painted pictures of animals
on the walls.

The world's highest mountain

The highest mountain in the world
is Mount Everest, 8 848 metres
(29,028 ft), in the Himalayas.

It is on the border
between Nepal and Tibet.

Everest

The summit was first reached
in May, 1953
by Sir Edmund Hillary
and Sherpa Tenzing.

Mountains of the Moon

These mountains are
in Central Africa,
almost on the Equator.

Although their summits
are always covered in snow,
there is jungle at their feet.

Alpine 3660 r

Heath 2896 r

Bamboo 2286 r

Rain
Forest 1676 r

Savannah

Ruwenzori Mountains (Mountains of the Moon)

A curious mountain

Here is a mountain
with a very strange shape.

It is Half Dome
in Yosemite National Park
in California, USA.

A round granite dome
was cut in half by a glacier.

Hydro-electricity

Mountain streams and rivers
are sometimes used
to make electricity.
Falling water is led by pipes
into a *power-station,*
where it turns *generators*
to produce the power.

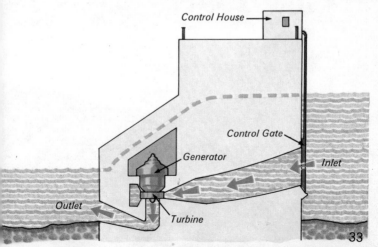

Control House

Control Gate

Inlet

Generator

Outlet

Turbine

Dams

The steep valleys
of some mountain areas
are sometimes blocked by *dams*
built of earth or concrete
so that a *reservoir*
(man-made lake) forms.

Water is often taken
from reservoirs in the mountains
to cities far away.

Mountain passes

For thousands of years
men have used *passes*
to cross mountain ranges.
Once men could only get through
with pack-horses and mules,
but now railways and main roads
use passes.

*Motorway through
the Great St Bernard Pass*

The Great Saint Bernard
and the Simplon
are important passes
through the Alps
between Switzerland and Italy.

Entrance to Mont Blanc Tunnel

Tunnels

Tunnels are now used
to enable roads and railways
to get through high mountain ranges.

The Mont Blanc Tunnel between France and Italy is 11 km (7 miles) long.

*Approaches to
Mont Blanc Tunnel*

Road		Railway	
Cable car		Houses	
Chair lift		Entrance to tunnel	

Cable cars and chairlifts

Cable cars are like buses
but hang from strong cables fixed
between the bottom of a mountain
and a point close to the summit.

They are pulled up and down
by electric motors.

Cable cars are used
in mountainous areas
in parts of France and Switzerland.

On a *chairlift* single seats
are fixed to a wire.
They are used to take skiers
to the ski-slopes.

Fell-walking

Many people enjoy
the beautiful scenery of mountains
and the challenge of reaching
a summit.

At weekends and in the holidays
many people go fell-walking.
(A *fell* is a steep mountainside
in the north of England.)

Rock-climbing

Rock-climbers tie ropes
around their waists
when climbing very steep rock faces.

Several climbers are roped together
then they climb a cliff or rock face
one at a time.

If one climber slips
the others can hold him.

Mountaineering

Climbing high or difficult mountains
is called *mountaineering*.

Ice axes are used to help climbers
in snow and ice.

Goggles may have to be worn
to protect climbers' eyes
from the glare of sunlight on snow.

Close to the summits
of the very highest mountains
there is less air than lower down.

Mountaineers on Everest
and other high peaks
have to take oxygen
in tanks strapped to their backs
to help them to breathe.

Ben Nevis

Snowdon

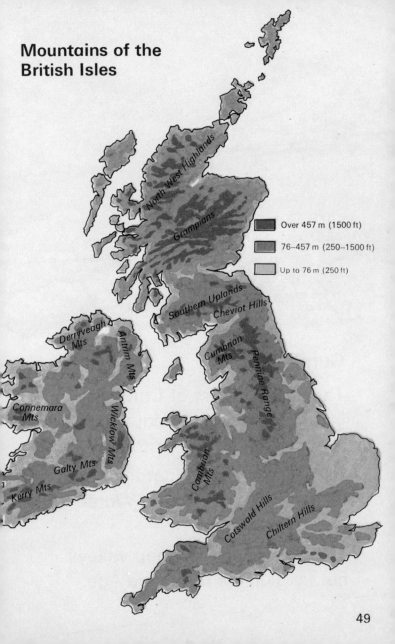

Mountains of the British Isles

North West Highlands

Grampians

☐ Over 457 m (1500 ft)

☐ 76–457 m (250–1500 ft)

☐ Up to 76 m (250 ft)

Southern Uplands

Cheviot Hills

Derryveagh Mts

Antrim Mts

Cumbrian Mts

Pennine Range

Connemara Mts

Wicklow Mts

Cambrian Mts

Galty Mts

Kerry Mts

Cotswold Hills

Chiltern Hills

49

Cumbria

View of Wast Water

Cumbria

The Lake District of Cumbria
is one of the most beautiful
mountain areas of Britain.

As well as high mountains there are
lakes such as Coniston Water
and Windermere.

These lakes are in deep valleys
cut by glaciers in the Ice Age.

The Scottish Highlands

The Highlands of Scotland
are the highest mountains in Britain.

On a few of them
there are snow patches
that lie for years at a time.

Ski-ing is usually possible
in winter in the Highlands.

The 731 metres (2399 ft) peak of Suilven

Index